THE LITTLE BOOK OF
FLORIOGRAPHY

Published in 2023 by OH!
An Imprint of Welbeck Non-Fiction Limited,
part of Welbeck Publishing Group.
Offices in: London – 20 Mortimer Street, London W1T 3JW
and Sydney – Level 17, 207 Kent St, Sydney NSW 2000 Australia
www.welbeckpublishing.com

ISBN 978-1-80069-539-9

Compiled and written by: Chloe Rodes
Editorial: Matt Thomlinson
Project manager: Russell Porter
Design: Ravina Patel
Production: Jess Brisley

A CIP catalogue record for this book is available from the British Library

Printed in China

10 9 8 7 6 5 4 3 2 1

THE LITTLE BOOK OF
FLORIOGRAPHY

THE SECRET LANGUAGE
OF FLOWERS

CONTENTS

INTRODUCTION

Flowers have been used to convey messages of love, friendship, celebration and condolence since time immemorial. In the Victorian era, when polite conversation was constrained by a strict moral code, flowers offered a way to reveal the secrets of the heart without having to utter a word.

Encyclopaedias with alphabetical lists of flowers and their associated meanings included feeling-to-flower translations, so that every emotion could be quickly transposed into floral form. If it's love you're keen to convey, your choices are endless, but more nuanced states of mind are taken care of too. Feeling forsaken? Turn to F — all you need are anemones.

The meanings the floral encyclopaedias gave to each flower were derived from a wide range of sources. Some borrowed from English and European folklore or Greek and Roman mythology. Some are associated with the plant's healing properties or use in traditional medicine. Others were inspired by the qualities or appearance of the flower, in keeping with the Christian custom of seeking the message of God in the form and attributes He'd bestowed on each of his creations.

The huge popularity of such collections suggests that almost every important Victorian exchange was conducted via posies and nosegays, but while it's difficult to know how much the system was really used, it's clear that a thorough knowledge of flowers and their symbolism was seen as a virtue.

In our age of direct, digital communication, *The Little Book of Floriography* offers a tiny taste of a past way of life. But it also attempts to provide ideas for those who'd like to learn the art of self-expression through flowers for modern times, sharing traditional meanings that still have resonance today and exploring the stories behind them.

CHAPTER
ONE

A POTTED HISTORY OF FLORAL SYMBOLISM

—✺—

"For the flowers have their angels... For there is a language of flowers. For there is a sound reasoning upon all flowers. For elegant phrases are nothing but flowers."

Christopher Smart
(*Jubilate Agno*, written 1759 to 1763)

ANCIENT ORIGINS

Ancient Egyptians made flower wreaths and garlands for the tombs of their loved ones, and decorated jewellery and ceramics, with the sacred lotus flower, which represented the sun god Ra, father of all creation.

In ancient Greece and Rome, flowers played an important symbolic role in society, both as a mark of status and to signify happiness and success. Laurel crowns were awarded to victorious athletes and floral headdresses were worn at weddings and exchanged as tokens of affection.

Chloris, Greek goddess of flowers (known as Flora in Roman legend), is said to have created many blooms, including the rose, larkspur and crocus, and appears in Botticelli's masterpiece *Primavera* surrounded by spring blooms.

Plants and flowers appear throughout Greek and Roman mythology, often springing up in the places where the blood or tears of the gods had been spilled.

"(While she spoke, her lips breathed out vernal roses): 'I, called Flora now, was Chloris."

Ovid's Fasti – Book five.

PRETTY AS A PICTURE

Flowers appear symbolically in religious paintings from the Middle Ages onwards. Red flowers, most often roses, represented the blood of Christ or symbolised his representatives on Earth — the monarchy. Edward III, King of England from 1327 to 1377, adopted the rose as his emblem.

Religious artworks often included lilies to represent the purity and maternal love of the Virgin Mary, such as Lorenzo Lotto's *Madonna and Child with Saint Jerome and Saint Nicholas of Tolentino*, painted in 1521.

By the middle of the Renaissance floral art was in full bloom and flowers and became the sole subject of many works of art. Paintings like the iconic *Bouquet* (1603) by Flemish artist Jan Brueghel the Elder are a celebration of the diverse beauty of nature's offering.

"Mary is the lily in God's Garden."

— Saint Bridget of Sweden
(1303 - 1373)

EASTERN INFLUENCE

While Renaissance Europeans were busy admiring floral still lifes, over in the Ottoman Empire, tulip mania had taken hold. The period from 1718 to 1730 became known the Tulip Era, and it was the height of fashion to cultivate them. The flowers became a potent symbol of status and wealth, with some individual flowers selling for the price of a house.

The fashion for floriography in the UK seems to have been imported from tulip-mad Turkey by English aristocrat, poet and feminist Lady Mary Wortley Montague, who accompanied her English ambassador husband to the country in 1717 and wrote home about the Eastern customs she witnessed.

Her letters, published with great popular appeal in 1763 after her death, described a rhyming mnemonic system called the *selam*, which paired objects with sentiments or feelings.

"There is no colour, no flower, no weed, no fruit, herb, pebble, or feather that has not a verse belonging to it, and you may quarrel, reproach, or send letters of passion, friendship, or civility, or even of news, without even inking your fingers."

– Lady Mary Wortley Montague

VICTORIAN VALUES

The seed of this idea for a means of wordless communication flourished in the fertile soil of Victorian polite society, where the outward expression of ardent feelings was seen as unseemly.

Just how often Victorian lovers really sent messages using the language of flowers is unclear, but the notion certainly captured the public imagination and it became a literary craze. The first dedicated book of floriography was *Le Langage des Fleurs* by Charlotte de Latour, in 1819, and almost 500 others followed, mostly combining the meanings with poetry and whimsical illustrations.

"The language of flowers has
recently attracted so much attention
that an acquaintance with it
seems to be deemed, if not an
essential part of a polite education,
at least a graceful and elegant
accomplishment."

Catherine H. Waterman
- *Flora's lexicon; an interpretation of the language and
sentiment of flowers; with an outline of botany, and a
poetical introduction, 1839.*

MODERN MEANING

Though many of the sentiments carried by flowers can now be quite freely conveyed in words, the appeal of symbolism is as strong as ever. The global floristry industry is booming too, estimated to be worth around 50 billion US dollars, and florists are keen to help customers imbue their blooms with deeper meaning.

Two recent royal occasions demonstrated that the language of flowers lives on. At the wedding of the Duke and Duchess of Cambridge, Princess Catherine reportedly based her choice of blooms for her bridal bouquet on their Victorian meanings and included myrtle, meaning hope and love, which appeared in Queen Victoria's own wedding bouquet in 1840.

At the state funeral of Queen Elizabeth II in September 2022, the choice of flowers and wreaths also conveyed a poignant message, including rosemary for remembrance and sweet peas, the late Queen's birth flowers, which mean thank you and goodbye.

CHAPTER

TWO

LOVE, FRIENDSHIP & ROMANCE

———❧———

By far the most popular sentiment to send
by way of floral messenger was love.
The blooms in this chapter can be used to
convey everything from maternal devotion
to passionate, romantic longing.

———❧———

Aster

(Michaelmas)

Aster

Love, daintiness

Named after the Greek word for star after the ways its point-tipped petals burst outwards from a central point, the aster's delicate form may be why it's symbolic of daintiness. One legend says asters sprang up where the tears of the Greek goddess Astara fell. Another associates it with the Greek goddess of love, which is why it's sometimes known as the herb of Venus.

ORIGINS

Asia and Europe, though the alpine aster is native to North America.

Banksia

(White honeysuckle / White bottlebrush)
Banksia

MEANING

Long-lasting love and endurance, renewal and rebirth

Indigenous peoples of Australia identified the energy-giving properties of this plant and drank the nectar or steeped the bark in water to make a reviving drink. The plant's woody, nutrient-storing base also means it's able to regenerate itself after wildfires, linking it to renewal and fresh starts.

ORIGINS

Native to the shrublands and rainforests of Australia and South Africa.

Camellia

Camellia japonica

MEANING

Longing for you (pink), you're a flame in my heart (red), you're adorable (white)

Wearing camellias became popular in Victorian England after the success of the 1848 Alexandre Dumas novel *La dame aux Camelias*, in which the heroine of the story wears one to indicate availability to her lovers. In China and Japan the flower is linked to eternal love because of the way the leaf-like protective structures are never parted from the petals, falling away along with them.

ORIGINS

Southern China, Vietnam, Japan and Indonesia, now grown widely in Australia, the US and Europe.

Carnation

Dianthus caryophyllus

MEANING

Fascination, female love, mother's love (if yellow: rejection)

Traditionally given on Mother's Day, the link to maternal love is thought to originate in the story that red carnations appear where Mary's tears made contact with the earth as Jesus was crucified. White carnations represent innocence and yellow carnations were a definite romantic rejection. Oscar Wilde made the unnaturally dyed green carnation a secret symbol of homosexuality in 1890s London.

ORIGINS

The Mediterranean region but grown all over the world.

Clover

(White)

Trifolium

MEANING

Think of me

White clover flowers are a symbol of ethereal beauty.
Arthurian legend tells the story of an ancient
Welsh goddess named Olwen who was so beautiful
that white clover sprang up wherever she walked.
Four-leaved clovers are also a symbol of good luck,
as they were said to be a sign of the presence of
fairies, who could bring good fortune.

ORIGINS

Temperate and subtropical regions
of the world.

Daisy

Bellis perennis

MEANING

Innocent love, childbirth and fertility

In folklore of numerous cultures the daisy is associated with the purity and innocence of childhood. According to Celtic legend, when an infant died, daises would spring up all over the land to help bring comfort to the bereaved. Since then, daises have been associated with innocence and purity.

ORIGINS

The oxeye daisy is native to Europe and Asia, while the English daisy is native to Europe.

Daffodil

Narcissus

MEANING

Regard, unequalled love

Given as a gift, daffodils represent love and
esteem, but the roots of this meaning are darker
than the sunny blooms suggest. In Greek legend,
Narcissus fell in love with his own reflection in a
pool of water and made him reject the love of
the nymph Echo. A narcissus sprang up when
he died and the flower is where narcissism —
excessive self-regard — gets its name.

ORIGINS

Northern Europe.

Dahlia

Dahlia pinnata

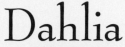

Lasting love and steadfastness devotion

The vibrant dahlia is linked to enduring affection because of its ability to bloom throughout the summer and on into autumn, even as the weather turns colder. This durability in spite of changing seasons means they're popular in wedding bouquets and for anniversaries.

ORIGINS

Native to the higher elevations of Mexico and Central America.

Forget-me-not

Myosotis

MEANING

True love memories, do not forget me

The name of this little blue flower makes it inseparable from the sentiment it expresses. It's been known as the forget-me-not since at least the Middle Ages, and appears in 15th century written records in Old French as 'ne m'oubliez mye'. A story about a German knight falling into a river as he tried to pick some for his true love and throwing them back to her calling "forget me not!" is appealing but apocryphal.

ORIGINS

Eurasia or New Zealand. A handful of varieties are also found in North and South America.

Gypsophila
(Baby's breath)
Gypsophila paniculate

MEANING

Innocence and lasting love

Known by the common name baby's breath for
it's cloud of airy white blooms and sweet, delicate
fragrance, it's associated with the purity of the infant
and is often given as a gift to congratulate new parents.
It's link to new beginnings means it summons the
promise of new love and is often chosen to decorate
wedding venues and included in bridal bouquets.

ORIGINS

Native to Europe and Asia but available
all over the world.

Heliotrope

Heliotropium arborescens

MEANING

Eternal love, devotion, faithfulness

Heliotropism is the turning of a living organism towards the sun and comes from the Greek — Hekio means sun and tropism is the turning towards or away from a source of heat or light. This tendency of the heliotrope flower to faithfully follow the sun as it moves across the sky is behind its reputation for unshakeable devotion.

ORIGINS

Some species are native to South America, others to Europe and found worldwide.

Hibiscus

Hibiscus rosa-sinensis

MEANING

Delicate beauty

For all their flamboyant splendour, the
hibiscus flower is best known for the brevity
of its existence — blooming for just a day before
withering and falling to the ground. The fleeting
nature of its radiance lends itself perfectly to its
meaning in floriography as a symbol of the
delicate and transient beauty of youth.

ORIGINS

China, but widely grown throughout
the tropics and subtropics.

Honeysuckle

Lonicera periclymenum

MEANING

Bonds of love

The spiralling vines of the honeysuckle, sometimes known as woodbine, are representative of the bonds of lasting love and commitment. Chaucer drew the symbolism of the plant in Troilus and Criseydei, in which pair are entwined in each other's arms like woodbine "aboute a tree, with many a twiste".

ORIGINS

Europe, Asia, the Mediterranean
and North America.

Hyacinth

Hyacinthus orientali

MEANING

Constancy

Ovid wrote that the Sun god Apollo was in love
with a mortal youth called Hyacinthus. The mortal
was a great athlete and the pair were playing sport
together when the young man was hit by Apollo's
discus and killed. In his grief and as a symbol of his
everlasting love, Apollo, possibly helped by the flower
goddess Chloris/Flora, had a beautiful flower spring
up in the spot where his lover fell.

ORIGINS

The Mediterranean region
and tropical Africa.

Ivy
Hedera

MEANING

Affection, friendship and fidelity

The curling tendrils of the ivy that cling to whichever tree, trellis or gatepost it grows against have associated the plant with the strong ties of friendship and the bonds of faithful love. In an early version of the old folk carol 'The Holly and the Ivy', the ivy represents the female, subservient to and dependent on the masculine holly.

ORIGINS

Eurasia and North Africa but now found across North America and Australia.

Jasmine

Jasminum

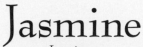

MEANING

Sweet love, amiability, grace, elegance

The meaning connected with this sweetly fragrant and graceful flower is thought to be derived from simple observation. The white star-like petals enhanced by dark green leaves and long, elegant vines that are easily trained to grow attractively around an arch convey a simple, uplifting refinement.

ORIGINS

Common jasmine is native to Iran. Other species come from across Eurasia, North America and Oceania.

Lily of the valley

Convallaria majalis

MEANING

Virginity, purity, heavenly

In Christian mythology the graceful bell-shaped flowers are known as 'our Lady's tears' — a reference to the tears shed by the Virgin Mary as her son Jesus died on the cross. From that time onwards lily of the valley was said to be used to gauge the purity of heart of the souls arriving at the gates of heaven.

ORIGINS

Inland Europe. An eastern species comes from East Asia and one species is native to the Eastern United States.

Morning glory

Ipomoea purpurea

MEANING

Affection

Flowering for just a single day, the star-shaped morning glory features in a Chinese folk tale in which a pair of lovers, Chien Niu and Chih Neu, are so distracted by their infatuation with each other than they forget their duties and are punished by being allowed to be together for only one day a year, when the morning glory is in flower.

ORIGINS

Central and South America, but at home across North America.

Pansy

Viola tricolor var. hortensis

MEANING

Thoughts

Pansies are the perfect gift to show someone they're in your thoughts. The flower's gently downward-tilted head is said to look like a person lost in reverie and its name comes from the French *pensée* meaning thought.
In *Hamlet*, Shakespeare has Ophelia clutching wildflowers as she pines for her dead father and says, "There's pansies, that's for thoughts…"

ORIGINS

Europe.

Rose

Rosa

MEANING

Love and devotion

Red roses are the universal emblem of love and
desire, and giving one (or a dozen!) is a clear
declaration of romantic intent. Other colours have
different meanings: pink roses show admiration,
white roses are symbolic of purity and innocence,
yellow roses represent friendship and happiness.

ORIGINS

Most of the hundred or so rose species that
are grown today can be traced back to Asia, though
some are native to North America and Europe.

Sage

Salvia

MEANING

Domestic virtues

One of the most prized of all domestic virtues was
a knowledge of plant medicine. The botanical name
of garden sage, *salvia*, comes from the Latin word
salvo, meaning to save or heal, and the plant has been
used as a herbal cure since the days of the ancient
Greeks. Dried sage was also burned to cleanse a space
of evil spirits and to purify the energy of the home.

ORIGINS

Indigenous to the Mediterranean region.

Speedwell

Veronica filiformis

MEANING

Feminine fidelity

The link to female faithfulness may come from a
Christian legend about St Veronica, who shares the
plant's botanical name. St Veronica is said to have
offered Christ her veil to wipe the mud from his brow
as he carried his cross to Golgotha. When he returned
it to her the fabric was marked with the outline of his
face and became a sacred relic.

ORIGINS

Native to Europe but grows in America.

Sweet William

Dianthus barbatus

Gallantry

Possibly named for William Augustus, Duke
of Cumberland, who displayed his gallantry by
leading the British in at the Battle of Culloden
in 1746. Others have suggested that the true
sweet William might have been Shakespeare.
The flower was, of course, linked to yet another
gallant William — the current Prince of Wales,
when it was chosen for the wedding bouquet of
Catherine, Duchess of Cambridge.

ORIGINS

Southern Europe and parts of Asia.

Tulip

Tulipa

MEANING

Passion, declaration of love

The period of the Ottoman Empire where
the language of flowers was born was known
as the Age of Tulips in honour of this sacred
flower. A Persian legend tells the story of Prince
Farhad, who was falsely told that his beloved,
a beautiful woman named Shirin, had died.
In his despair he took his own life, only for
Shirin to discover him and kill herself.
Red tulips sprang up where their blood fell.

ORIGINS

Turkey and central Asia.

Violet

Viola

MEANING

Watchfulness, modesty, faithfulness

The purple/blue petals of English, or wood-violets turn slightly inwards and grow on slender green stalks that bend under the weight of the bloom, suggestive of a head bowed in modesty. Their link to purity was strengthened by Shakespeare's use of them in *Hamlet*. When Ophelia dies her brother Laertes says:

'Lay her i' th' earth,
And from her fair and unpolluted flesh
May violets spring...'

ORIGINS

Europe, other species come from Asia.

Yarrow

Achillea millefolium

MEANING

Everlasting love

Yarrow was historically used in European folk
traditions as a tool for love divination. Young
women would put a sprig of the flowers under
their pillow to summon a dream of their future
spouse or use it in rituals to tell if the object of
their affections returned their devotion.

ORIGINS

Eurasia — from the UK to China
and across North America, Australia and
New Zealand.

Zinnia

Zinnia elegans

MEANING

Thoughts of absent friends, lasting affection

Bright and cheerful zinnia flowers come in pink, purple, red, white, and yellow. Their jolly appearance and ability to reseed quickly, filling a bed with vibrant colour, made them the perfect representation of friendship. And from Victorian time right up to the enforced separations of the Coronavirus pandemic, they've been used to bring comfort when friends are apart.

ORIGINS

The southern United States, Mexico and Chile.

CHAPTER

THREE

HEALTH, WEALTH & HAPPINESS

---◆---

The gift of a bright bouquet is the perfect
way to wish someone a speedy recovery after
illness, to congratulate a hard-won success
or celebrate a happy occasion. The species
in this chapter offer a wide range of ways to
say it with flowers.

---◆---

'The Earth laughs in flowers.'

Ralph Waldo Emerson
(*Hamatreya*, 1847)

Angelica

Angelica archangelica

Inspiration

As its name suggests, this plant is linked in
Greek mythology to angels. It's meaning may
derive from the legend of a monk who was inspired
with a life-saving idea after dreaming of an
archangel who told him that the plant could be
used to cure the plague. Angelica was already used
medicinally in China and was an ingredient in
many natural remedies during the plague years.

ORIGINS

Northern Hemisphere
(sub-arctic regions).

Basil

Ocimum basilicum

MEANING

Good wishes (though also, contrarily, hate)

Italian folklore links basil to affection and generosity — a sprig of basil was a sign of romantic intentions. In the language of flowers, however, basil can also signify hate. This may spring from its association in Ancient Greece with the Latin word *Basilicus* or *Baselisk*, the name of a terrible and much feared mythical beast.

ORIGINS

Native to India and grown across Europe and Asia.

Bay

Laurus nobilis

Glory

Bay was symbolic of the Greek god Apollo,
who was in love with a nymph named Daphne.
She begged her father to turn her into a tree to put
an end to his pursuit of her. Legend has it that she
was turned into a bay tree and Apollo wore a wreath
made from her branches. Bay laurel crowns were
given to the victors of athletics contests and are still
associated with achievement and glory.

ORIGINS

Native to the Mediterranean region.

Blackthorn

Prunus spinosa

MEANING

Faith and hope

Jesus's crown of thorns is said to have been
a wreath of blackthorn, which has made the
tree symbolic of enduring faith and hope.
In Celtic folklore, throwing a blackthorn branch
to the ground would make a thick forest grow,
providing protection from enemies.

ORIGINS

Europe and western Asia.
It can also be found in New Zealand
and eastern North America.

Bluebell

Hyacinthoides non-scripta

MEANING

Humility, constancy and everlasting love

Blue flowers in general symbolise loyalty and devotion. According to old English folklore, if you're able to turn a bell-shaped bluebell flower inside out without tearing the petals, you're sure to one day be united with your true love.

ORIGINS

The ancient woodlands of Western Europe.

Chamomile

Matricaria chamomilla

Energy or strength in adversity

Chamomile's symbolism may stem
from its reputation as a plant doctor —
it's known to revive other blooms planted
nearby and is traditionally used in a
healing tea, said to soothe the mind and
body and encourage the return of vitality.

ORIGINS

Europe, North Africa and Asia and now
grown widely in North America.

Chrysanthemum
Chrysanthemum

MEANING

New life, optimism and joy, also circle of life – death

In Asia where the flower is native, chrysanthemums are associated with youth and revered for their health-giving properties when drunk as tea. Their autumn blooming could be linked to circle of life. In Europe, though, they've come to be seen as a symbol of sorrow, though the seemingly opposite interpretations may in fact be linked. Chrysanthemums were left on war graves to commemorate bright young lives cut short.

ORIGINS

China, eastern Asia and north-eastern Europe.

Cosmos

Cosmos

Order and harmony

These star-shaped flowers are named for the Greek word *kosmos*, which translates as "beauty" or "harmony". One story goes that they were given this name by Spanish priests who grew the flowers and noted the perfectly ordered arrangement of the petals, seeing them as representative of the order and harmony of the universe.

ORIGINS

Mexico and Central and South America.

Crocus

Crocus sativus

Cheerfulness, youthful gladness

One of the first flowers to emerge in springtime, these plants beat the cold by keeping their female reproductive parts below ground, sending up a long floral tube so that they can flower even through frost and snow. Their bright petals in purple, yellow and white are celebrated as an early sign of spring, linking them to fresh beginnings and the joy of new life.

ORIGINS

The Mediterranean, Asia, and much of Europe.

Edelweiss

Leontopodium nivale

MEANING

Courage, devotion

The name of this white, wool-like flower comes
from the German for noble (*edel*) and white
(*Weiss*). It's an emblem of courage and devotion
because reaching the high alpine pastures
where it blooms requires both these attributes
in abundance. Those able to return with the
gift of an edelwise for their beloved had truly
proved their bravery and dedication.

ORIGINS

Alpine areas of Europe and
South America.

Eucalyptus

Eucalyptus regnans

MEANING

Protection and healing

Eucalyptus has been used in traditional
Aboriginal medicine for centuries and it's known
for its antiseptic and anti-inflammatory properties.
The plant's leaves and essential oils are used to
treat gastrointestinal problems, wounds, join and
muscle pain and respiratory illness.
In a bouquet it conveys hopes for healing.

ORIGINS

Australia. Some species grow in the
most temperate parts of Europe.

Fern

Polypodiopsida

MEANING

Magic, enchantment

Beliefs about the supernatural abilities of
this ancient plant arose because it seemed to
reproduce by magic. Ferns release spores rather than
flowering, so some early investigators thought their
seeds might be invisible. This sparked the superstition
that ferns could confer invisibility on anyone who
held it. In Shakespeare's *Henry IV*, the highwayman
Gladshill reassures his accomplice that they won't
be seen with the line: 'we have the receipt of fern
seed; we walk invisible'.

ORIGINS

All continents except Antarctica.

Gladioli

Gladiolus

MEANING

Integrity, Strength and Victory

Known as the flower of the gladiators, with whom it shares its title, the long, blade-like appearance of the flower stem gave rise to its name, which means sword in Greek. One legend that may lie behind its meaning claims they sprang from the earth when two young Thracian warriors, who'd been captured by the Roman army and become friends, refused to fight each other and were both put to death.

ORIGINS

South Africa but also found in the Mediterranean.

Goldenrod

Solidago

MEANING

Encouragement, good fortune

Used in Native American plant medicine for centuries, Goldenrod gets its Latin name from a combination of the words "make" and "whole". It's association with good fortune could also stem from Chinese beliefs that its golden colour would encourage wealth and riches.

ORIGINS

North America, though a few species grow in Europe and Asia.

Iris

Iris

MEANING

Faith, wisdom, hope, valour

Named after the Greek goddess of the rainbow for their spectacular colours, irises have been revered as a symbol of power since ancient times and appear alongside royalty in frescos painted in the 2nd century BCE. The Egyptians decorated royal sceptres with the flower's image and used its root stems to make incense for religious ceremonies. The trio of petals were said to represent faith, wisdom and valour.

ORIGINS

Europe and Asia.

Hawthorn

Grataegus Oxyacantha

MEANING

Hope and strength

The dense, spiked branches of the hawthorn are naturally associated with strength, since they enable the plant to thrive in the most exposed of environments. The additional meaning — hope — may come from the fact that the Greek god of marriage and the wedding song, Hymenaios, traditionally carried a flaming torch made from hawthorn to light the way of newlyweds towards a long and happy union.

ORIGINS

Europe, North America and Asia.

Hollyhock

Alcea rosea

MEANING

Ambition and fecundity

The natural hardiness of this tall and proud-looking plant gave rise to its link with ambition. Traditionally seen as a mark of high social status, traces of the flowers have been found in the coffin of Tutankhamun. They were also celebrated for their ability to reproduce readily, with a round seed box falling to the soil as the parent plant begins to fade, which makes them a potent symbol of fertility.

ORIGINS

Native to China but cultivated widely the world over.

Kangaroo Paw

Anigozanthos

MEANING

Strength and good health

The vibrant anigozanthos, with its
eye-catching paw-shaped flower head, is a symbol
of strength because of its incredible resilience.
It's broad, underground stem system means that
the plant is able to survive drought and even bush
fires. It's been used in traditional Aboriginal
medicine for thousands of years.

ORIGINS

Western Australia.

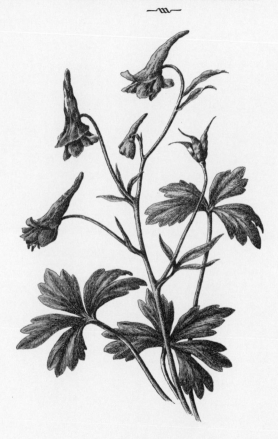

Larkspur

Delphinium

MEANING

Open heart, levity, lightness

There can be few more uplifting sounds than the song of the ascending sky lark. The meaning given to the delphinium comes from its link to this joyful bird. Its common name was given because its seed pods resemble the spurred foot of the lark, whose trilling mating call heralds the end of winter and the promise of spring.

ORIGINS

Northern hemisphere, most notably in the mountainous African tropics.

Lilac

Syringa vulgaris

MEANING

Joy of youth, innocence and purity

The innocence of a young wood nymph named Syringa is the source of the lilac's hidden meaning. According to legend, she was turned into the reed-like flower to escape the attentions of Pan, who tried to embrace her but was left holding reeds that made a beautiful sound as he sighed with regret (AKA pan pipes). Her purity preserved, the delicate purple blooms became associated with her attributes.

ORIGINS

Eastern Europe and milder parts of Asia.

Lily

Lilium lancifolium

MEANING

Happiness, wealth, confidence and pride

Like roses, the precise meaning of lilies is
dependent on their colour. Yellow signifies sunny
happiness, the golden lustre of orange blooms
made them symbols of wealth and prosperity.
In Japan, where the flower is native, the language
of flowers is known as *Hanakotoba*, and tiger
lilies are given to celebrate milestones such as
graduations or new jobs.

ORIGINS

East Asia, including China and Japan.

Lotus flower

Nelumbo nucifera

MEANING

Purity, enlightenment, self-regeneration, and rebirth

Associated with the Egyptian sun god Ra,
the Lotus flower was sacred and represented the
divine. The flower's extraordinary behaviour -
it closes and sinks beneath the surface of the river
at night only to rise again at dawn and open its
bright petals — make it synonymous with rebirth.

ORIGINS

East Asia, South Asia, Southeast Asia
and probably Australia.

Magnolia

Magnolia

MEANING

Nobility, love of nature

The appearance of this broad-leaved ornamental tree with its wide-spreading branches and sculptural, waxy white flowers has made it representative of nobility. The state flower of Louisiana and Mississippi, it's associated with dignity and stability. The plant is native to China, where it's often given on teachers' day as a mark of respect and admiration for the noble profession of teaching.

ORIGINS

Asia, the Americas, and most of northern Europe.

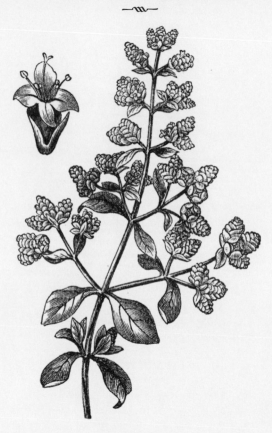

Marjoram

Origanum majorana

MEANING

Joy and happiness, blushes

Said to have been willed into existence by the Greek goddess Aphrodite as a symbol of joy in her garden, wild marjoram is often known as oregano in Europe. It's a European folk custom to wear a sprig of the herb on the day of your wedding to invite joy and happiness into the marriage.

ORIGINS

The Mediterranean and western Asia, also naturalized in Mexico and the United States.

Nasturtium

Tropaeolum

MEANING

Patriotism, conquest, victory in battle

Nasturtium was given its Latin name *tropaeolum*, meaning trophy, because its leaves are shaped like shields, and the shield of defeated enemies were traditionally taken by the victors as an emblem of their success in battle. This association, along with the helmet-like shape of the flowers, makes it the perfect plant with which to convey patriotism or to congratulate someone on a hard-won success.

ORIGINS

Native to South and Central America.

Peony

Paeonia lactiflora

MEANING

Bashfulness

Peonies can take three or four years to
flower and there may be years when buds form but
never open. The conditions have to be exactly right.
A Chinese legend tells the story of an Empress who
was impatient for spring and called on the flower
goddess to make the flowers open even though it
was still winter. She agreed and the next morning
every flower bloomed, except for the shy peony.

ORIGINS

Native to Europe and Asia.

Poppy

Papaver

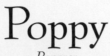

$\boxed{\text{MEANING}}$

Consolation

Poppies have symbolised sleep and eternal rest
since ancient times, its seeds used to make
the sleep-inducing narcotic opium. In Greek
mythology, brothers Hypno, god of sleep,
and Thanatos, god of death, wore crowns of
poppies. For the last hundred years, the poppy
has been used as a mark of remembrance for
those who've lost their lives in war.

$\boxed{\text{ORIGINS}}$

Southern Europe, North Africa
and milder regions of Asia.

Rosemary

Salvia rosmarinus

MEANING

Remembrance

Used as a memory aid since ancient times, the aromatic herb was thought to sharpen the brain, which meant it was seen as useful for aiding the memory. In medieval times it was used for embalming bodies, which led to its association with mourning the dead. In *Hamlet*, Shakespeare gives the bereaved Ophelia the line: 'There's rosemary, that's for remembrance.'

ORIGINS

The Mediterranean region.

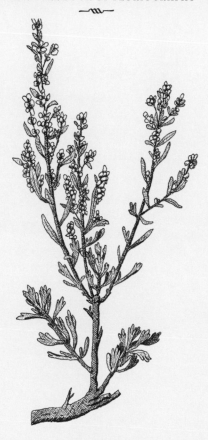

Sagebrush

Artemisia tridentate

Wisdom and clarity

Sagebrush was used by Native Americans for its medicinal and anti-microbial properties, and for purifying and cleansing people's bodies, souls and houses. After such a cleansing, it is easier to start afresh, with new insight and clarity. And because of the harsh conditions it grows in, sagebrush can also represent strength and resilience.

ORIGINS

The semiarid plains and mountain slopes of western North America.

Sweet pea

Lathyrus odoratus

MEANING

Blissful pleasures,
good-bye,
thank you for a lovely time

These delicately frilled flowers were a favourite of
Queen Victoria and became wildly popular in the
Victorian era. Given at weddings, they were associated
with enjoyment and happy occasions. They were
also used to express thanks on parting and a wreath
containing them graced the coffin of Elizabeth II,
who grew them in her gardens at Balmoral.

ORIGINS

Sicily, Cyprus and Southern Italy.

Tickseed

Coreopsis

MEANING

Always cheerful

The sunny faces of the golden tickseed flower represent abiding bright spirits, a meaning enhanced by their ability to thrive in dry, rocky landscapes. Used as a tea in traditional plant medicine, the plant was said to cure stomach problems and restore strength. Its vibrant yellow colour was also used as a dye to bring a cheering splash of colour to fabrics.

ORIGINS

North America and Central America.

Thyme

Thymus vulgaris

MEANING

Courage, strength

The word thyme stems from the Greek, *thymon*, meaning to offer or burn incense, and its meaning may come from the linked word *thymos*, meaning spiritedness. Virgil recommended it to counter fatigue, and renowned 17th century herbalist Nicholas Culpeper recorded the herb's use for strengthening the lungs. In the Middle Ages a sprig of thyme was given to encourage bravery in knights as they set off to fight in the crusades.

ORIGINS

Southern Europe
and Mediterranean regions.

Wattle

Acacia

MEANING

Chaste love, protection

The national flower of Australia is known for providing protection from the sun's unrelenting gaze. It's offering of shelter is also seen in Bible stories: in Exodus acacia is the wood that Moses was told to use when building the Ark of the Covenant, the gold-plated chest that contained the two tablets with God's laws inscribed on them. The plant's sensitivity — it shrinks from touch — may be behind its association with chastity.

ORIGINS

Native to Australia.

Wild lupine

Lupinus

MEANING

Determination, imagination and creativity

These narrow-tipped pillars of petals prefer soil
that's low in nutrients and are known to flourish
even in areas that are parched or damaged.
This ability makes them ideal for conveying
a determination of spirit and as a symbol of
the power of the imagination to conjure a rich
landscape out of meagre resources.

ORIGINS

Western parts of North America.

CHAPTER

FOUR

POISON IVY
PLANTS WITH LESS
POSITIVE ASSOCIATIONS

—⁓—

Despite their colourful appearance and
pleasing scent, not all blooms are bright and
cheerful in the language of flowers. The
suggestions in this chapter cover those species
whose message is more sombre.

—⁓—

'Sweet is the rose,
but grows upon a briar.'

— Edmund Spenser
(Sonnet XXVI 1552–1599)

Acanthus

Acanthus mollis

MEANING

The fine art, artifice

Though in modern times artifice implies
trickery or deception, in the era of the
language of flowers, it meant simply artificial
or manmade. The meaning may have its
origins in the use of the acanthus plant as a
decorative symbol in Roman and Byzantine
temples, where their sculptural beauty meant
they were considered as works of art.

ORIGINS

North Africa, Asia and Australia,
with three species native to southern Europe.

Amaryllis

Amaryllis

Pride

With their tall, sturdy stems and large,
usually deep-red petals, the amaryllis stands
proud above the other flowering plants.
Also considered as a symbol of strength and
determination, the gift of them in a bouquet
could be read two ways, either as a sign of
admiration, or to convey a signal that
the receiver is too proud.

ORIGINS

South Africa but now cultivated
all over the world.

Anemone

Anemone

MEANING

Forsaken

In Greek mythology anemones are linked to the tragic love story of goddess of love Aphrodite and the mortal Adonis. Adonis was killed by a rival while out hunting and Aphrodite tried to bring him back to life. The flowers are said to have sprung from where his blood mingled with her tears and fell onto the earth.

ORIGINS

Temperate and subtropical regions of all continents except Australia, New Zealand and Antarctica.

Begonia

Begonia

Beware

These bright flowers are more delicate than
their exuberant colours suggest and in colder
climates only grow well in greenhouses with
plenty of shade. Some flower dictionaries
also link them to dark thoughts. Their
vulnerability, along with their preference for
dark places, may be behind the rather ominous
meaning.

ORIGINS

Central and South America,
Africa and Asia.

Belladonna

Atropa belladonna

MEANING

Silence

Also known as deadly nightshade, this highly toxic plant was used by the ancients as a poison — ingesting even small quantities of its roots, leaves or dark berries can be fatal. The Latin name of its genus links the plant to Atropa, who, in Greek mythology, was one of the three goddesses of fate responsible for choosing the manner of a mortal's death and for severing the thread of life.

ORIGINS

Southern Europe to Asia.

Butterfly weed

Asclepias tuberosa

MEANING

Let me go/leave me

This pretty, bright orange flower seems a strange choice to convey a message of severance, but it may have got its meaning from its use as a flower of remembrance. Left on the graves of lost loved ones, it's associated with painful partings. Though, in the strictly governed rules of Victorian communication, it may also have proved useful in the delicate matter of breaking off an unwanted romantic attachment.

ORIGINS

North America.

Candytuft

Iberis

MEANING

Indifference or stoicism

The sweet-sounding name of this pretty
ornamental plant belies its hardiness. This candy
has nothing to do with sugar but comes from the
former name of the capital city of Crete, a rocky
Mediterranean island where the flower is native.
Its meaning may stem from its indifference to the
conditions it grows in — able as it is to flourish
quite contentedly in tough terrains.

ORIGINS

Southern Europe.

Carnation
(Striped)
Dianthus caryophyllus

MEANING

Disappointment, regret

Striped carnations are genetically altered hybrids and in the language of flowers, they have their own translation. According to an Italian folk tale, a young maid called Margherita gave a white carnation to her beloved, Orlando, when he set off to war. A year later it was returned it to her after Orlando's death, stained with his blood. The seeds from the flower grew into red-and-white striped blooms, symbolising regret that love can't be shared.

ORIGINS

Cultivated across the world.

Clematis
(Evergreen)
Clematis vitalba

MEANING

Poverty

The evergreen vine's association with poverty isn't
well documented but may have to do with its efforts
to climb and thrive by clinging to sturdier plants and
trees. The wispy strands of pale grey that grow from
its fruit earnt it the nickname Old Man's Beard.
According to folklore, those in need of ropes and
baskets wove them from the feathery threads.

ORIGINS

North America. Others are native
to temperate parts of Asia like Japan
and much of China.

Columbine

Aquilegia

MEANING

Anxious, trembling

Another flower whose various meaning depended
on the colour of the bloom – red columbines
symbolise anxiousness and trembling, while blue
petals signify both a message from the unconscious
and foolishness and folly. Both meanings may come
from the Celtic tradition of ingesting the seeds and
roots to bring on trance-like states, believing that
they opened a pathway to other worlds.

ORIGINS

Western North America.

Crab apple blossom

Malus sylvestris

MEANING

Ill nature

The white and pink blossom of the crab apple
tree looks a million miles from ill-natured, but
the fruits of many species are known for their
sharp, bitter taste and can only be eaten in jams.
The seeds and stems can also be mildly toxic
and, like ordinary apples, contain cyanogenic
glycosides... yep, that's cyanide. Poisoning is rare
but they can leave you with a sour stomach.

ORIGINS

The woodlands of Europe.

Cyclamen

Cyclamen

Resignation, diffidence, goodbye

This cheery looking perennial's unusual timing is behind its rather sombre meaning. It blooms during the winter months and goes into dormancy in the summer, which married it with endings, barrenness and sterility. The sight of their bright petals fading in spring, just as other wild flowers burst into bloom, linked them with decline. The bulbs and root stems are also toxic, which increased their association the long goodbye.

ORIGINS

Middle East and southern and central Europe.

Foxglove
Digitalis

MEANING

Insecurity, secrets

Every part of the foxglove is poisonous,
containing toxic compounds that can kill
if ingested in large enough amounts. Its other
nicknames, witch's gloves and dead man's
bells, hint more precisely at its dark side.
The flower also evokes the secrecy of the
faery folk — fox is thought to be a contraction
of "folk's" — the enchanted pixies, elves and
imps that made mischief with anyone entering
their magical domain.

ORIGINS

Britain and Western Europe.

Geranium

Geranium

MEANING

Folly, stupidity

Also known as cranesbills for their slender, beak-shaped fruit, the geranium may have come to represent stupidity through its link to this innocent bird. In Aesop's fable 'The Crane and the Wolf', the gullible crane foolishly removes a bone from the wolf's throat on the promise of a reward, which of course, never comes. Some sources attribute the meaning to Victorian snobbery, which viewed the simple plants as fit only for a lower class of gardener.

ORIGINS

Subtropical southern Africa.

Lavender

Lavandula angustifoli

Distrust

In spite of the many medicinal benefits of this beautifully scented plant, in the language of flowers it meant distrust. An apocryphal legend says the asp that killed Cleopatra with its poisonous bite was hidden in a lavender bushel, and though this is untrue, vipers are rumoured to rest in the shade between plants in lavender fields, which perhaps gives reason enough to be wary.

ORIGINS

Native to countries bordering the Mediterranean.

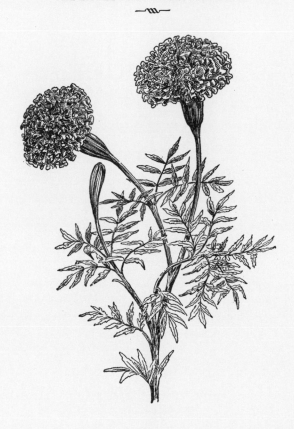

Marigold

Tagetes

 MEANING

Grief

Just as mourners bow their heads in times of
sorrow, the marigold hides its face at dusk,
closing its flowers if there's cloud cover or if
storms threaten. They only open again when the
sun is out and high in the sky. In springtime,
when the flowers are in bloom, dew collects
inside the folded petals during the night and
drips to the ground in the morning like tears
when the blossoms re-open.

ORIGINS

Southwestern North America,
tropical America and South America.

Poison ivy
Toxicodendron radicans

MEANING

Death

The Latin name is a clue to the plain
language spoken by this notorious plant.
The toxin behind its ominous message
is urushiol, a clear compound in its sap
that causes a painful and itchy rash on
the skin if touched. Even dead leaves
can cause a reaction, and though external
irritation isn't a medical emergency,
if eaten, it can be fatal.

ORIGINS

North America and Asia.

Rhododendron

Rhododendron

Danger, beware

Produced as an effective defence against insects, the toxins in rhododendrons are called grayanotoxins, which can cause poisoning with numerous alarming effects if either the plant or its by-products are consumed. They can slow the heartbeat, block electrical signals in the heart, cause vomiting and nausea, and induce a delirium associated with shifts in consciousness. A kind of honey made from the nectar is tellingly nicknamed "mad honey".

The northern hemisphere, south-east Asia and Australia.

Snapdragon

Antirrhinum

[MEANING]

Deception or presumption

Snapdragon flowers conceal a macabre secret — their seedpods are shaped like tiny human skulls. According to folklore, hiding a snapdragon about your person makes you seem enchanting and affable, even if you're actually anything but. They were sent as messages of forbidden love in dalliances of deceit.

[ORIGINS]

Western North America and the western Mediterranean region.

Sunflower
(Tall)
Helianthus

MEANING

Haughtiness, false richness

The striking, showy appearance of the tall
sunflower meant that it was attributed with the
undesirable qualities of superiority and arrogance.
The rich yellow of its petals so celebrated for its
sunniness today was seen in Victorian times as a
brassy facade, promising false riches. The gift of
one of these would surely have been enough to bring
the most high and mighty down a peg or two.

ORIGINS

North and South America.

Tansy
Tanacetum vulgare

$$\boxed{\text{MEANING}}$$

Hostile thoughts, declaring war

Yellow and sweet scented but harbouring
a deadly weapon, tansy was traditionally
used in herbal medicine for the toxic
chemical thujone. Its meaning comes
from its ability to make the body hostile
to other life — it was used to bring on
abortions and to treat intestinal worms.

$$\boxed{\text{ORIGINS}}$$

Miler areas of Europe and Asia.

Thistle

Cirsium

MEANING

Unwanted intrusion and misanthropy

Stepping barefoot onto a thistle gives as clear a message as anything to keep off. The plant's spiny leaves – a defence against being eaten by grazing animals – won it a reputation for a dislike of humankind. A bouquet containing a thistle could be read either as an accusation of a prickly nature or as a warming not to come any closer.

ORIGINS

Europe, Asia and North America.

"There is a language, little known,
Lovers claim it as their own.
Its symbols smile upon the land,
Wrought by nature's wondrous hand;
And in their silent beauty speak,
Of life and joy, to those who seek
For Love Divine and sunny hours
In the language of the flowers."

—The Language of Flowers,
London, 1875